INDIGENOUS BIOGRAPHIES

Wilma Mankiller

Political Leader

FOCUS READERS BEACON

by Katrina M. Phillips

www.focusreaders.com

Focus Readers is distributed by North Star Editions:
sales@northstareditions.com | 888-417-0195

Produced for Focus Readers by Red Line Editorial.

Photographs ©: Tom Gilbert/Tulsa World/AP Images, cover, 1; Peter Turnley/Corbis Historical/VCG/Getty Images, 4; Buddy Mays/Alamy, 6; Carol M. Highsmith/Library of Congress, 8; National Archives, 11; J. G. Domke/Alamy, 13; Warren K. Leffler/Library of Congress, 14; Robert W. Klein/AP Images, 16; Michael Wyke/Tulsa World/AP Images, 19, 29; Barry Sweet/AP Images, 21; Marcy Nighswander/AP Images, 22; Don West/AP Images, 25; Shutterstock Images, 27 (coin), 27 (background)

Library of Congress Cataloging-in-Publication Data
Names: Phillips, Katrina M. author
Title: Wilma Mankiller: political leader / by Katrina M. Phillips.
Description: Mendota Heights, MN: Focus Readers, [2026] | Series: Indigenous biographies | Includes bibliographical references and index. | Audience: Grades 2-3
Identifiers: LCCN 2025012053 (print) | LCCN 2025012054 (ebook) | ISBN 9798889985037 hardcover | ISBN 9798889986577 paperback | ISBN 9798889985662 pdf | ISBN 9798889985358 ebook
Subjects: LCSH: Mankiller, Wilma, 1945-2010--Juvenile literature | Cherokee women--Biography--Juvenile literature | Indian activists--Biography--Juvenile literature | LCGFT: Biographies | Literature.
Classification: LCC E99.C5 P45 2026 (print) | LCC E99.C5 (ebook) | DDC 973.04/975570092 [B]--dc23/eng/20250416
LC record available at https://lccn.loc.gov/2025012053
LC ebook record available at https://lccn.loc.gov/2025012054

Printed in the United States of America
Mankato, MN
012026

About the Author

Dr. Katrina M. Phillips (Red Cliff Ojibwe) is a writer, researcher, and history professor. She's written several children's books about Native histories and cultures, including *Indigenous Peoples' Day* and *I Am on Indigenous Land*. She and her husband live in Minnesota with their two sons and their goofy dog.

Table of Contents

CHAPTER 1

Making History

Wilma Mankiller made history in 1987. The Cherokee Nation chose her as its next **principal chief**. Mankiller became the first woman elected to this office.

Wilma Mankiller pushed for better health care and education. She wanted to create more jobs for Cherokee people.

John Ross (statue) was the first principal chief of the Cherokee Nation. He served for nearly 40 years.

The Cherokee elected their first modern principal chief in 1970. Since then, the Cherokee had gained more land. They had written a new **constitution**. They had built health care systems. They had improved their economy, too.

Mankiller was following in many Cherokee women's footsteps. She was part of a long line of women who served the Cherokee people.

Did You Know?

Some Cherokee women were honored with the name "Beloved Woman." They led the Women's Council. They also sat on the Council of Chiefs.

CHAPTER 2

In California

Wilma Pearl Mankiller was born on November 18, 1945. She grew up in Tahlequah, Oklahoma. This town is on the Cherokee **reservation**. Wilma's father was Cherokee. Her mother was Dutch and Irish.

Tahlequah is the capital of the Cherokee Nation.

The Mankillers hunted and fished to feed the family. They gathered wild plants. They grew vegetables, too. Life was not always easy.

In 1956, the US Congress passed a new law. It was called the Indian **Relocation** Act. Government officials hoped the law would force

Did You Know?

More than 100,000 Native people were relocated between 1952 and 1972.

In the 1950s, the US government got many Native people to relocate to big cities such as Denver, Colorado.

Native people off reservations. They wanted Native people to move to larger cities. They promised good jobs and good housing.

The Mankillers wanted to find a better life. They left Tahlequah shortly before Wilma's 11th birthday. They moved to the San Francisco Bay Area in California. But the jobs didn't pay well. The family's apartment was too small. Kids teased Wilma and her siblings because they were Native. They made fun of their last name.

However, the Mankillers were not alone in the Bay Area. Many other Native families had come

In 1950, about 2,000 Native people lived in the Bay Area. By the 1980s, more than 35,000 did.

to California, too. Wilma's family started going to the American Indian Center. They found friends and community there. It was an important place for many Native people in the Bay Area.

WE MARCH FOR INTEGRATED SCHOOLS NOW!
WE DEMAND DECENT HOUSING NOW!
WE DEMAND AN END TO BIAS NOW!
WE DEMAND AN END POLICE BRUTALITY NOW!
RIGHTS NOW!
JOBS and FREEDOM
FREEDOM IN '63

CHAPTER 3

Finding Her Voice

Wilma Mankiller finished high school in 1963. She got married soon after. She had two daughters before she was 21. She loved her daughters. But she wanted to be more than a housewife.

By the 1960s, the civil rights movement had been pushing for justice for several years.

The occupation of Alcatraz Island lasted for 19 months. It drew attention around the world.

The 1960s were a time of change across the United States. Native **activists** took over Alcatraz Island in 1969. They were **protesting** the US government. They opposed its treatment of Native people.

Four of Mankiller's siblings took part in the protests. Mankiller was inspired. She raised money to support the **occupation**. She also helped secure money for the Pit River Tribe. And she helped lead the Native American Youth Center in Oakland.

Did You Know?

Black Americans, Chicanos, and Asian Americans also worked for **civil rights** in the 1960s.

Mankiller wanted to keep working for Native rights. But her husband preferred a wife who stayed home. They got divorced in the 1970s.

Mankiller and her daughters moved back to Oklahoma. She started working for the Cherokee Nation. She raised money for tribal programs. She also planned to finish her college degree.

Cherokee leaders were impressed. They asked her to help with other projects. In 1983, the principal

In 1985, the principal chief stepped down. Mankiller went from deputy to principal chief.

chief came to her. He asked her to run as his **deputy** chief. They won the election. Mankiller became the nation's first female deputy chief. Then she was elected principal chief in 1987.

TOPIC SPOTLIGHT

Native Activism

Native people have always fought for their rights. This movement grew in the 1960s and 1970s. Many protests took place in the Pacific Northwest. In 1964, Native people in the Puget Sound created the Survival of American Indians Association. They worked to protect Native fishing rights.

Other groups followed. For example, Ojibwe and Dakota people in Minneapolis, Minnesota, formed the American Indian Movement in 1968. They wanted to help Native people in the Twin Cities.

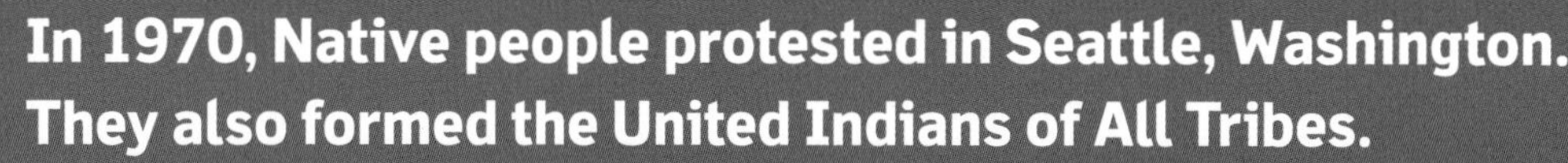

In 1970, Native people protested in Seattle, Washington. They also formed the United Indians of All Tribes.

CHAPTER 4

A Legacy of Leadership

Wilma Mankiller spent 10 years as principal chief. Afterward, she kept advocating for the Cherokee. She also continued to support Native people across the United States.

Principal Chief Mankiller speaks with the Choctaw Nation's leader during a US Senate hearing in 1989.

Mankiller served in a variety of roles. She taught at Dartmouth College. She went on a speaking tour. She spoke about health care and women's rights. She also talked about tribal **sovereignty**.

Mankiller received many honors for her leadership. President Bill Clinton gave her a major award in 1998. It was the Presidential Medal of Freedom. This is the highest honor for someone who did not serve in the military.

In 1998, Mankiller spoke along with Angela Davis (left) and Gloria Steinem (right) at a women's rights event.

Mankiller died on April 6, 2010. She had dealt with health problems her whole life. More than 1,000 people went to her funeral, including President Barack Obama.

The funeral was a celebration of Cherokee culture. Principal Chief Chad Smith honored Mankiller and her family. Smith gave her family the Cherokee Nation's Medal of Patriotism. The medal usually goes to Cherokee veterans. Mankiller was the first person to receive the award

Did You Know?

Wilma Mankiller was honored on a 2022 quarter. It was part of the American Women series.

Mankiller's quarter displays the seven-pointed star of the Cherokee Nation.

who had not served in the military. She had helped change the course of history.

Focus Questions

Write your answers on a separate piece of paper.

1. Write a letter to a friend about Wilma Mankiller's life.
2. Would you have relocated like Wilma's family did? Why or why not?
3. When was Mankiller elected principal chief?
   - **A.** 1956
   - **B.** 1987
   - **C.** 1995
4. Why were Cherokee leaders impressed with Mankiller?
   - **A.** They saw her family move to California.
   - **B.** They saw the work she was doing for her people.
   - **C.** They saw her focusing on being a housewife.

5. What does **inspired** mean in this sentence?

*Mankiller was **inspired**. She raised money to support the occupation.*

A. moved to do something
B. losing money
C. opposed to making change

6. What does **veterans** mean in this sentence?

*The medal usually goes to Cherokee **veterans**. Mankiller was the first person to receive the award who had not served in the military.*

A. people who were not in the military
B. people who had never been honored
C. people who were in the military

Answer key on page 32.

Glossary

activists
People who take action to make social or political changes.

civil rights
Rights that protect people's freedom and equality.

constitution
A document laying out a nation or state's basic beliefs and laws.

deputy
Second in command in a leadership role.

occupation
Taking control of a place as a form of protest.

principal chief
The leader of the Cherokee Nation.

protesting
Gathering to show disagreement with something.

relocation
The process of moving to a new place.

reservation
Land set aside by the US government for a Native nation.

sovereignty
The power to make rules and decisions without being controlled by another country.

To Learn More

BOOKS

Buckley, Patricia Morris. *The First Woman Cherokee Chief: Wilma Pearl Mankiller.* Penguin Random House, 2023.

Sánchez Vegara, Maria Isabel. *Wilma Mankiller.* Frances Lincoln Children's Books, 2022.

Sorell, Traci. *She Persisted: Wilma Mankiller.* Philomel, 2022.

NOTE TO EDUCATORS

Visit **www.focusreaders.com** to find links and resources related to this title.

Index

Answer Key: 1. Answers will vary; 2. Answers will vary; 3. B; 4. B; 5. A; 6. C